ANONYMITY

BOOKS IN THE LIBRARY FUTURES SERIES

ALA**✴**
Neal-Schuman
CHICAGO | 2019

ALA CENTER FOR THE FUTURE OF LIBRARIES

ANONYMITY

ALISON MACRINA AND TALYA COOPER

LIBRARY FUTURES **1**

ALISON MACRINA is the founder and director of Library Freedom Project and a core contributor to The Tor Project. Her work aims to connect privacy and surveillance to larger struggles for justice. She has been awarded the Free Software Foundation's Award for Social Benefit and the New York Library Association's Intellectual Freedom Award, and she was a *Library Journal* Mover and Shaker.

TALYA COOPER is an archivist based in New York City. Previously, she was the digital archivist at the Intercept, where she managed the Snowden archive, and the archive manager at StoryCorps. She has written and presented about the intersections of archival ethics, privacy, and security.

© 2019 by the American Library Association

Extensive effort has gone into ensuring the reliability of the information in this book; however, the publisher makes no warranty, express or implied, with respect to the material contained herein.

ISBNs
978-0-8389-1633-9 (paper)
978-0-8389-1932-3 (PDF)
978-0-8389-1930-9 (ePub)
978-0-8389-1931-6 (Kindle)

Library of Congress Cataloging in Publication Control Number: 2019019623

Cover design by Kimberly Thornton. Composition by Alejandra Diaz in the Adobe Garamond Pro, Vista Sans and Vista Slab typefaces.

♾ This paper meets the requirements of ANSI/NISO Z39.48-1992 (Permanence of Paper)

Printed in the United States of America
23 22 21 20 19   5 4 3 2 1

ALA Neal-Schuman purchases fund advocacy, awareness, and accreditation programs for library professionals worldwide.

CONTENTS

FOREWORD

BY MIGUEL A. FIGUEROA

Center for the Future of Libraries
American Library Association

THERE'S A COMMON THROUGH LINE IN TODAY'S TECHNO-logical trends and developments that promise improved convenience and efficiencies: they trade on access to a broadening universe of public and private information and data.

An increase in surveillance systems (an estimated 245 million professionally installed video surveillance cameras were active and operational globally in 2014),[1] the movement toward "smart cities" (cities of all sizes are embarking on projects that will deploy technologies to collect and transmit information to improve city operations),[2] the ubiquity of voice recognition devices (the number of Amazon Echo installed bases in the U.S. grew to more than 30 million by 2017),[3] and other technology trends will ultimately exacerbate privacy concerns. As our concerns shift from the personal to the public, the resulting conversations may likewise swing from threats to privacy to the end of anonymity.

In *Anonymity,* Alison Macrina and Talya Cooper guide readers from privacy, a core value for our profession, toward a related appreciation and understanding for anonymity. They show how anonymity, the obscuring or withholding of identity, has implications for individuals, communities, and the libraries that serve them. While anonymity has that very real connection to our profession's fundamental value for privacy, the conversations library professionals must have regarding anonymity extend far beyond our users' experiences in or even with the library. Our communities exist in a world where lived experiences

---

1. https://technology.ihs.com/532501/245-million-video-surveillance-cameras
   -installed-globally-in-2014.
2. www.usmayors.org/wp-content/uploads/2018/06/2018-Smart-Cities-Report.pdf.
3. www.kleinerperkins.com/perspectives/internet-trends-report-2018.

in public and online have become a valuable source of data for governments, corporations, and other agents to collect and leverage.

Through "Understanding Anonymity," Alison and Talya help readers understand anonymity in our users' broader lives by providing an immersive vision for how anonymity plays out today and how it might continue to shift for the future. Their insight for how anonymity connects with library values centers the discussion in terms of both privacy and equity, recognizing that different users have varying needs for anonymity at distinct points in their lives.

From practical policies and procedures to technological interventions and educational instruction, "Anonymity in Libraries" shows how libraries can model anonymity's benefits and liabilities in a changing society. The Tor Project,[4] the LibraryBox Project,[5] and other initiatives show the promising directions that help ensure privacy while centering anonymity.

In "For the Future," Alison and Talya imagine new opportunities for libraries to advocate by standing up when policies or practices threaten individual rights to privacy and anonymity, educate by raising community awareness of the changing natures of privacy and anonymity, and implement spaces and technologies that make accommodations for anonymity while preserving security for staff and users alike.

It was Alison's work with the Tor Project and the Library Freedom Project that helped me better understand anonymity's significance for libraries. Here, with Talya, whose important advocacy in archives informs this work, they make clear why thinking about our futures requires thinking beyond the normal scope of our users' experiences in the library to also consider the library in the lives of our users. I continue to be inspired by leaders like Alison and Talya whose clarity of vision brings our traditions and values boldly into what may likely be a challenging future.

---

4. www.torproject.org.
5. http://librarybox.us.

ACKNOWLEDGMENTS

THANK YOU TO THE LIBRARIANS WHO TOOK THE TIME TO speak to us about their experiences: Melissa Morrone, Chuck McAndrew, Shannon O'Neill, Bobbi Newman, James Hutter, TJ Lamanna, Lucas Gass, and Rob Caluori.

Talya would like to thank the Intercept's Research Team from 2016–2019: Research Director Lynn Dombek, Erinn Clark, Akil Harris, Westley Hennigh-Palermo, Sheelagh McNeill, Margot Williams, John Thomason, Mariam Elba, and Alleen Brown.

Alison would like to thank all the librarians who have worked with Library Freedom Project over the years, especially the members of Library Freedom Institute. She is also grateful to her fellow Core Contributors at The Tor Project.

UNDERSTANDING ANONYMITY

THE NEW NORMAL

YOU STEP OUTSIDE INTO THE BALMY SEPTEMBER evening, walk across the church parking lot, and open the door to your car with a sigh. Turning the red chip over as you hold it above the steering column, you think about the relativity of time. The past thirty days have been longer than any others you can remember, and it feels like actual years or even lifetimes have passed. You wouldn't have made it this far without the program and the ability it gives you to speak freely and openly among these strangers, protected by the practice of using only first names. You pop the coin into your wallet and pull out your smartphone, nonchalantly scrolling through Facebook, when something makes you pause over the "People You May Know" suggestions. Facebook has suggested that "You May Know" Bill R. and Mike M. from the meeting, except Facebook is telling you their full names, their family members, where they're employed, and all their likes. And it's telling them the same about you.

We live in an age of ubiquitous surveillance: many tiny pieces of our lives are constantly recorded, shared, and stored. We offer some of this information voluntarily in exchange for various services, while private corporations, law enforcement, and government intelligence agencies collect more of it almost invisibly. Libraries should be particularly concerned about the new norms of surveillance. Privacy has been one of the ALA's Core Values of Librarianship[1] since their adoption in 1939. Librarians have long recognized the relationship between privacy and intellectual freedom; when we lack privacy, we can't have intellectual freedom, because we are less likely to read, write, and research freely when we fear that we're being watched.

Privacy and anonymity are not synonymous, though. Privacy means that you get to control what information about you is shared. Anonymity, privacy's stricter cousin, means that in a given situation, no one knows your real identity. So why isn't this book about "privacy" rather than "anonymity," which sounds like something for secret agents and Internet trolls? Given the current surveillance environment, we believe that anonymity is as important for librarians to understand, support, and promote as privacy in general. Privacy has become a hot topic in libraries, with privacy-focused projects springing up all over the place—from the Data Privacy Project in New York City, to Library Freedom Project (of which one of this book's authors is founder and director), to the San Jose Public Library's Virtual Privacy Lab.[2] Anonymity, on the other hand, is still something of a curiosity for librarians—it is certainly present in the current fervor about privacy, but it is harder to understand and advocate for. We'd like to talk about why anonymity has value on its own, because of the ways that identity is weaponized

---

1. http://www.ala.org/advocacy/intfreedom/corevalues.

2. https://www.sjpl.org/privacy.

for surveillance purposes and monetized by big corporations. In order to understand why anonymity matters, it's important to know just what is happening to our data on the Internet these days.

PEOPLE YOU MAY KNOW

The opening story about Facebook identifying people who were anonymous to each other through its "People You May Know" tool is based on a real incident. Reporter Kashmir Hill heard innumerable anecdotes from users who'd found fellow patients of their psychiatrists and other attendees of support groups among their suggested friends, and reached out to Facebook to ask how and why the company was exposing these people to each other. Facebook admitted to using location services to "suggest friends."[3] After significant backlash, the company reversed course and denied that it had used location services as a factor in suggesting friends, finally admitting it had run "a small test to use city-level location to better rank existing [People You May Know] candidates."[4] In short, location services had been used to suggest friends at least for a portion of users for a period of time, which could have sufficed to de-anonymize a group of people in serious need of anonymity. Facebook also openly uses contact information (which it strongly suggests you upload upon creating an account) to chain users together. That function can be great if a user wants to get in touch with someone a mutual friend introduced them to at a networking event and that person appears as a "Person You May Know." But if two people have the same AA sponsor or mental health practitioner in their contacts and Facebook links them together and suggests that they "friend" each other, the "People You

---

3. https://splinternews.com/facebook-is-using-your-phones-location-to-suggest-new
   -f-1793857843.
4. https://splinternews.com/facebook-says-it-did-a-test-last-year-using-peoples-loc
   -1793857952.

May Know" feature starts to feel more like a gross violation of privacy, a nonconsensual disclosure of their identity.

This is not the only time Facebook has gotten in trouble for harmful or exploitative data practices. In 2018 alone, Facebook faced privacy scandal after privacy scandal,[5] and we can't point the finger at Facebook alone. The private companies that dominate the Internet collect huge amounts of data on users as part of their standard practice. The services we use for keeping up with friends, staying on top of the day's news, and for various modern conveniences like banking or shopping also track us elsewhere all over the Web, on our phones, and in the real-life spaces we inhabit. Big data is the business model, and there are few if any limits on how big these companies are able to get and how much information they're able to collect. Yet with so much precious information currency being generated, stored, and sold, data security seems like an afterthought. Major data breaches, from Equifax to Yahoo to the U.S. Office of Personnel Management, have spilled out the private details of hundreds of millions of people, and such breaches are all too commonplace.

All the data collected, stored, and often lost by private companies makes ubiquitous government surveillance easier than ever, coupled with the fact that law enforcement and intelligence agencies' surveillance budgets get larger and less transparent every year.[6] In 2013, Edward Snowden showed us how pervasive mass surveillance has become in the twenty-first century. We are subject to a byzantine network of entities that are capable of surveilling our every move and communicating it to each other, often in real time. The digital devices that have come to power our lives also generate a nearly invisible data trail that has proven

---

5. https://www.techrepublic.com/article/facebook-data-privacy-scandal-a-cheat-sheet/.

6. https://www.washingtonpost.com/wp-srv/special/national/black-budget/?noredirect=on.

highly valuable to all of those private entities. The combination of more data and better surveillance mechanisms means that the average computer user can expect that her most private information is in the hands of dozens of private companies and government apparatuses, regardless of who she is or what she's been doing. Those people whose data seems more interesting to law enforcement or intelligence agencies can expect even more surveillance, possibly with serious consequences.

To understand how all-encompassing this network is, let's imagine a person traveling from Los Angeles to Portland, Oregon. She wants to take her beloved St. Bernard, so instead of flying, she buckles in for a minimum fifteen-hour drive, during which she'll stop for a couple of meals and snacks, a whole lot of coffee, gas, and a number of rest stop breaks for the dog and herself. We all anticipate some level of surveillance, from a full-body scan to profiling in the TSA line, when we fly. But even this road trip will subject our two travelers to scrutiny by a vast number of public and private entities.

Leaving Los Angeles, this woman's car will be recorded by a number of cameras, some operated by law enforcement agencies and some operated by private companies: for instance, some repossession agencies use cameras and Automated License Plate Readers (ALPRs) to track car owners who are behind on their payments. Our traveler may also pay tolls with an electronic toll collection device, which records the time and location of the payment. This data could potentially be shared with a fusion center, a hub where federal agencies like the Department of Homeland Security and the Department of Justice collaborate with local, state-level, and tribal law enforcement. On her tiring drive, our traveler will pass no fewer than four fusion centers, from the Los Angeles Joint Regional Intelligence Center to the Oregon Titan Fusion Center in Salem. Local police also use ALPRs and compare the data they take in to registries that attempt to match the plate number to crimes as serious as Amber Alerts and as banal as unpaid parking violations. As of 2011, 71 percent of police departments reported using this technology.[7] Moreover, we know that the traveler voluntarily exposes herself to all kinds of tracking through her cell phone's apps: the maps app she's using to find the quickest detours, the restaurant app that remembers her interest in vegetarian food, and the dating app she swipes idly while her dog sniffs around at the rest stop. The phone itself serves as a tracking device—it functions by sending electromagnetic signals to the closest cell tower, and law enforcement or a wireless carrier can easily find the location of the most recent cell tower a phone has "pinged."

These are just the technologies we know are in use, though. Let's say the traveler's license plate bears a similarity to the license plate number of a car that was used in a crime. Potentially, law enforcement at a fusion center could access the footage from a CCTV camera at a rest stop and use facial recognition—a technology that's advancing so rapidly it will soon be able to identify masked protesters[8]—to determine whether or not the traveler is the person they have in mind. Other technologies can pull in data about her and her trip through means that we don't even know about yet. And this is all before our traveler posts on Facebook about her trip, which will make the whole story openly available to law enforcement, third-party apps she's unwittingly allowed to access her posts, and anyone else who might be interested in her whereabouts.

7. https://www.theatlantic.com/technology/archive/2016/04/how-license-plate-readers
-have-helped-police-and-lenders-target-the-poor/479436/.

8. https://www.theverge.com/2017/9/6/16254476/facial-recognition-masks-diguises-ai.

How did we come to live in a terrifying sci-fi novel? Information has become a precious commodity that is fought over by major corporations, intelligence agencies, law enforcement, nation states, and hackers. Technology has permeated our lives by creating conveniences that would have seemed to belong to a far-distant future as recently as just ten years ago. As consumer devices have grown increasingly sophisticated, so have police surveillance capabilities. The regulatory environment has been wheezing to keep up as digital giants like Google and Amazon vacuum up smaller companies and expand their reach into our day-to-day lives, and intelligence agencies add zeroes to their enormous budgets. The future as seen by the master dystopian author Philip K. Dick is here. What does a digital resistance movement look like? And how can librarians take part in it?

We began by talking about how a private company can sabotage the much-needed anonymity of one of its users. While the potential for anonymity, and privacy in general, is deeply threatened by this *Black Mirror* episode of a future that we're now living in, librarians and libraries can play a pivotal role in allowing our communities to use the Internet without unregulated private companies and powerful government agencies learning who they are and what they're doing. When it comes to the Internet, anonymity is autonomy. As with other kinds of freedoms, people can abuse tools that grant them anonymity and free them from the consequences that voicing opinions and acting under their "real" identities might have. But anonymity also has the potential to make the Internet into a more democratic place, giving voice to the powerless rather than to the powerful.

The idea that anonymity can help someone safely and confidently express their beliefs long precedes the Internet. As librarian Chuck McAndrew of the Lebanon Public Library in New Hampshire points out, "When I talk about anonymity with people, I like to point out that Thomas Paine published 'Common Sense' anonymously originally. That was one of the most influential books that spawned the American Revolution. From the start of this country, anonymity has had a very important point in the [democratic] process." Anonymous whistleblowers have played a key role in exposing abuses of power and miscarriages of justice. As an employee of the RAND Corporation in the late 1960s and early 1970s, Daniel Ellsberg began to believe that the United States' involvement in the Vietnam War was unjust, and so he anonymously leaked the "Pentagon Papers," a set of documents that showed the Johnson Administration had systematically deceived the American people about the war. His leaks were later published by the *New York Times*. These documents helped turn public opinion against the war and established a legal precedent for newspapers to publish leaked materials. Ellsberg's need for anonymity was situational and temporary; he turned himself in not long after leaking the papers to Neil Sheehan at the *New York Times*. But anonymity gave him the cover he needed to get the job done. A lower-stakes recent example is the beloved Italian author Elena Ferrante, who writes pseudonymously because, she says, she wishes "to liberate myself from the anxiety of notoriety and the urge to be a part of that circle of successful people."[9] When a journalist attempted to unmask her by trawling through tax and financial records, the literary world responded to his would-be expose with outrage and indignation,[10] questioning how revealing the identity of an author who so values her anonymity would add to readers' appreciation or understanding of her work. Similarly, many street artists operate anonymously in order to avoid prosecution for work

---

9. https://www.vanityfair.com/culture/2015/08/elena-ferrante-interview-the-story-of-the-lost-child-part-two.

10. https://www.npr.org/sections/thetwo-way/2016/10/03/496406869/for-literary-world-unmasking-elena-ferrantes-not-a-scoop-its-a-disgrace.

that, while technically illegal, has high value both for the communities where their art appears and, for some, in the art market.

In the past few years, archivists and oral historians who work with collections that represent marginalized and vulnerable communities have also thought through the value of anonymity for the people their collections represent. It can be difficult to strike a balance between ensuring that personal accounts and stories are preserved for the historical record and guaranteeing the safety of individuals who go on the record. During the 2015 Society of American Archivists annual conference in Cleveland, where a police officer had recently been acquitted of manslaughter after shooting two unarmed black people, a group of archivists recorded a set of oral histories. In the wake of the acquittal, the group wanted to create a collection—now known as the People's Archive of Police Violence in Cleveland[11]—to describe the grinding regularity of police violence and harassment that many people of color in Cleveland experience. The archivists understood that talking about experiences with the police could be challenging for many in the community: some people were involved in ongoing court cases, while others feared retaliation for speaking out against the police. Consequently, the archivists allowed many of their participants to record their stories anonymously, or to use only a first name or pseudonym. Historians tend to view anonymous accounts as less valuable to the record because they can't be verified. The creators of this archive acknowledge this critique in the online collection description by stating that "despite the anonymity, this collection will be useful for the larger and complex narratives of police violence in Cleveland that it conveys." In essence, they used anonymity as a way to tell a story both in individual voices and as an aggregated account, without putting anyone at risk.

---

11. http://www.archivingpoliceviolence.org/collections/show/2.

HOW DO YOU GET TO BE ANONYMOUS?

It's hard to be anonymous, though. In the early days of the Internet, many users embraced online identities divorced from their in-real-life (IRL) ones: think about AOL and GeoCities screen names like Book-Lover465 or BostonTerrierLuv. Since Facebook began to require that users provide a "real" first and last name and a valid phone number, and flags users who have not provided that information, it's become both technically difficult, and in some contexts, socially unacceptable, to be anonymous online. In 2010, Mark Zuckerberg famously told a journalist that "having two identities for yourself is an example of a lack of integrity."[12] Although Facebook softened its stance and does not require full names for some of its other products (Instagram, for instance), it suspends the accounts of users who have either been reported or algorithmically determined to be using fake names. Transgender rights activists, among others, have organized against this policy.[13] As people transition or explore their gender identities, they often choose to go by new names. They also may want to shield themselves from discovery by family members or colleagues who don't know about their new identity. Far from reflecting "a lack of integrity," these names can represent online identities that are truer to people's real selves than their state-assigned identities, in a space that allows them to express those identities safely.

A number of quasi-anonymous apps have seen brief swells in popularity, including the "gossip" apps YikYak and Whisper. It may be that in the post-Snowden era, more people in the mainstream are attracted to the idea of anonymity than ever before. People have come to realize

---

12. https://venturebeat.com/2010/07/21/live-blog-zuckerberg-and-david-kirkpatrick-on
    -the-facebook-effect/.
13. https://www.theguardian.com/world/2017/jun/29/facebook-real-name-trans-drag
    -queen-dottie-lux.

anonymity's power in a networked world, a power that some Internet users see fit to abuse. The infamous imageboards 4chan and 8chan require no registration and keep no memory, and have served as the breeding grounds[14] for pernicious movements like GamerGate, a 2014 campaign of harassment against women in the gaming industry so vicious that several of its targets went into hiding, fearing for their lives. These imageboards are also frequently credited with the rise of the "alt-right" and resurgent white supremacist movements in the United States.[15] These Internet movements use anonymity to create real-life chaos for people through the practice of "doxing"—finding, publishing, and using someone's personal information without their consent. In a heralded 2010 TED Talk, 4chan founder Chris "m00t" Poole described the imageboard's success in unmasking the identity of an animal abuser, to applause from the audience. We now tend to see this tactic as harmful, as doxing often represents an attempt to intimidate or silence activists or other politically outspoken people. Women, LGBTQ people, and people of color are much more likely to be targeted. Behind the shield of anonymity, malicious Internet users send threats of physical harm and employ tactics like "swatting" (calling in false reports of serious crimes so that a horde of law enforcement officers show up at a target's home or workplace) in an effort to intimidate them. In an interview published on NPR, Robin Nelson, a black feminist and biological anthropologist, expressed deeply mixed feelings about exposing her identity online:

> I am finding that this kind of conservative self-policing is not worth
> it—issues around black women's health and safety, personal safety
> and policing in black communities, issues of sexual harassment and
> assault more broadly have to be discussed by everyone, particularly

14. https://www.dailydot.com/layer8/8chan-pedophiles-child-porn-gamergate/.
15. https://www.theguardian.com/technology/2016/dec/01/gamergate-alt-right-hate-trump.

by those who have any kind of inclination, privilege, or platform. Thus, while I am finding myself speaking out more about these issues—I know I do so with considerable risk to my career and perhaps my physical safety. I have been trolled on Twitter following tweets about sexism and sexual harassment in academe, and racist policing in black communities. I have genuine concerns about being doxxed.[16]

Using her own identity online allows Nelson to speak up for—and from the perspective of—several marginalized groups. At the same time, it makes her vulnerable to online harassment from anonymous Twitter trolls, many of whom tend to be white men, coming from a position of relative privilege.

But there are easily just as many examples of anonymity for good, some even using the same outlets as the bad. Many people know about the hacker collective Anonymous, a leaderless online movement that uses anonymity to perform "ops" or mass protest movements. They came to fame after Project Chanology,[17] an op directed at exposing the pernicious aspects of the Church of Scientology. They organized online, conducting DDoS (distributed denial of service) attacks to bring down Scientology websites, and also held in-person protests. A significant amount of this organizing happened on 4chan, the same anonymous imageboard where GamerGate and the alt-right developed.

Researchers and academic librarians reading this text may have heard of Sci-Hub, a database of academic papers created as a form of protest against the exorbitant fees that journals charge libraries and scholars for access. Its creator, Alexandra Elbakyan, founded the service in frustration

---

16. https://www.npr.org/sections/13.7/2015/02/26/389233371/a-toxic-stew-risks-to
    -women-of-public-feminism.
17. http://www.newsweek.com/anonymous-takes-scientology-93883.

when, as a student at an under-resourced university in Kazakhstan, she could not access the materials she needed for her work.[18] Today, the site has over 150 million papers. If a user requests an article that is not currently in Sci-Hub's database, the service uses a set of library credentials—donated by anonymous academics who support the site's mission to provide free access to information—to log into a library database and retrieve the file. Sci-Hub's success depends on a broad, anonymous community of people with a shared interest and belief in the freedom of information. Many librarians support Sci-Hub's guerrilla open-access work because they see libraries compelled to funnel increasing percentages of their budgets into expensive subscriptions for academic journals.

Many news organizations, like the Intercept, where one of the authors formerly worked, receive anonymous submissions of leaked materials through instances of the open-source platform SecureDrop (which is also made possible by Tor onion services). Whistleblowers have used this platform to send in materials that exposed covert government programs and corporate malfeasance. Revelations that came about from anonymous submissions to Secure Drop have led to public uproar, lawsuits, and legislative change. Subsequent government prosecution of several anonymous leakers reflects the serious threat that these whistleblowers face, and the strength of de-anonymizing technologies that the government has in its arsenal.

As these examples show, anonymity allows for more open sharing of information and for individuals to speak freely without fear of repercussions, abilities we consider key components of a democratic society.

---

18. https://www.washingtonpost.com/local/this-student-put-50-million-stolen-research -articles-online-and-theyre-free/2016/03/30/7714ffb4-eaf7-11e5-b0fd-073d5930a7b7 _story.html?utm_term=.94566b422754.

Given the overarching surveillance of everyday life we've described, though, how can anyone be anonymous? Total anonymity may indeed be impossible, due to the information-sharing networks that span government and corporate entities. The 2016 Equifax data breach perfectly exemplifies the near-impossibility of entirely concealing your real identity. Most Americans require credit as a necessary condition of living in our society; that credit rating must be tied to a government-assigned identification number, which itself is a requirement for receiving all kinds of other services. When a private corporation irresponsibly exposes this data, your identity as a consumer and as a citizen—as well as any other data linked to those profiles, like health information that you access using your Social Security number—becomes vulnerable to any number of bad actors.[19] Remember our earlier description of fusion centers, and how information from corporate sources can combine with government data to track individuals as they move through the world. Anonymity does indeed seem impossible. However, it is possible to be anonymous in *some* contexts *some of the time*, even if the best you can do is make it harder for an attacker to de-anonymize you.

ANONYMITY LOVES COMPANY

Achieving any level of anonymity begins with understanding the potential risks and adversaries you will face. In the security world, this is known as *threat modeling,* or *risk assessment*. Threat modeling takes into account your adversaries (people or entities who threaten you or your community), their capabilities, what you want to protect from them, what will happen if you fail to protect yourself, and where you have left yourself and your data open to risk. This is an incredibly important

---

19. https://www.wired.com/story/the-equifax-breach-exposes-americas-identity-crisis/.

skill for librarians to master, given the variety of people who come into our buildings and use our services. We must understand the different threats faced by a Muslim teen, a leftist activist, and a woman escaping domestic violence, so that we may shape our policies and practices to their needs. In doing so, we should adopt an "intersectional framework." Kimberlé Crenshaw, the legal scholar who coined this term, says that intersectionality is "a lens through which you can see where power comes and collides, where it interlocks and intersects." As we think about risk assessments, we must acknowledge the power relationships at play—how powerful entities are using some of the most sophisticated surveillance technology the world has ever seen, and how people with multiple marginalized identities are put at greatest risk by these new technologies. In this way, we can begin to make the institutions where we work safer for the people who are most impacted by the loss of privacy.

As part of its Surveillance Self-Defense initiative,[20] Electronic Frontier Foundation provides a list of questions to help construct a threat model:

- What do I have that is worth protecting?
- Who do I want to protect it from?
- How likely is it that I will need to protect it?
- How bad are the consequences if I fail?
- How much trouble am I willing to go through to prevent these consequences?

Here's one way to think about a threat model as it applies to digital information and anonymity.

As a teenager attending a religious high school, one of this book's authors had a lot of questions about gender and sexuality that her school's health classes did not address. I knew the Internet could provide

---

20. https://ssd.eff.org/en.

some answers, but our school's computer lab had a firewall that blocked certain words and terms, and at home, I shared a computer with my whole family. At this positively prehistoric time, browsers did not have incognito mode, so I would log on to our home PC in the evening, seek out whatever information I wanted, and carefully, manually delete the browser history, cookies, and log files at the conclusion of every session. I calculated that if I forgot to delete all of this data when I finished and someone else discovered what I'd been exploring, the worst thing that could happen would be an awkward conversation with my relatively open-minded parents or a hearty teasing from my younger brother.

But what about a queer teen with a family who deems their sexuality sinful, who is interested in these same topics? Would they have risked using a computer in their home? If this teen slipped up and forgot one step of the process of deleting their Internet trail, its discovery could lead to a deprogramming camp, public shaming, or even expulsion from their family. Although the asset they need to protect (their Internet search history) and the people they wish to protect it from (their family) precisely match this author's, their threat model differs significantly because of the additional risk they take on in pursuing this necessary and valuable information. This hypothetical example shows the utility of anonymity and a case in which having "multiple" identities—or being anonymous—is hardly the threat that Mark Zuckerberg deems it to be. Closeted youth aren't anonymous to their parents at the breakfast table or to their friends at school, but they also don't need to expose their Internet searches or blog posts to their entire IRL social circle.

In discussing threat models, we also must emphasize that the full force of the surveillance state primarily strikes low-income communities and communities of color. On a daily basis, this might come in the form of cameras or watchtowers in and around housing projects and in "high crime areas" (typically low-income neighborhoods populated by people of color). The scholar and writer Arun Kundnani frames this issue within the digital realm as follows:

> The post-Snowden debate also has not been able to grasp the way that race is central to surveillance. If you look at how the NSA is responding to the allegations, it's by saying, "You, as an average American guy, don't have to worry about surveillance. We're only going after the bad guys who are the terrorists, the foreign spies, and so forth." This is a racially coded way of reassuring the majority of Americans. That part of it never gets discussed. We much prefer this "Big Brother" account of NSA surveillance, where everyone is equally under surveillance, but that's not how it works. The danger of describing the NSA in terms of a Big Brother image is that you end up saying that the problem is mass surveillance of everyone, which can carry the implication that "targeted" surveillance is fine. But, in practice, "targeted" surveillance could mean collecting data on everyone in Yemen, or the entire Muslim population of the US.[21]

Kundnani here explains that framing surveillance as ubiquitous avoids a necessary conversation around its essentially racist dimension. As we think about the kinds of adversaries who might want to de-anonymize our patrons, we must keep this bias in mind.

Police informants and private security companies have infiltrated Muslim-American student groups[22] and groups protesting the Dakota

---

21. "Total Policing and the Global Surveillance Empire Today: An Interview with Arun Kundnani," by Jordan T. Camp and Christina Heatherton, in *Policing the Planet*, ed. Jordan T. Camp and Christina Heatherton (Brooklyn, N.Y.: Verso, 2016), 92.
22. https://www.nytimes.com/2017/03/06/nyregion/nypd-spying-muslims-surveillance -lawsuit.html.

Access Pipeline,[23] and the NSA has monitored the e-mail communications of leaders in Muslim civil-rights organizations.[24] Less dramatically but no less impactfully, young people are surveilled by parents who might check their phones or install tracking software on their computers and by school computers which log web traffic. Although young people can be menaced by predators and scam artists online, they also need privacy and unfettered access to information, in no small part because increasingly, they're at the forefront of activist campaigns. Combine these factors and imagine the threat model for a teen working on a Black Lives Matter campaign, using social media and text messages to organize. After Snowden, the public rightly became outraged at the idea of "mass government surveillance," but targeted surveillance has become just as omnipresent for members of marginalized groups and political dissidents.

Although focusing on potentially vulnerable members of our patron communities can help us make a clearer case for anonymizing technologies, these are not the only people who stand to benefit from learning about and using these tools and practices. Many of us need anonymity and don't necessarily realize it, because we haven't thought expansively either about our own threat models or about the threat models of the circles in which we move. One of this book's authors often asks friends to use Signal—perhaps the most reliable app for encrypted texting and calling—rather than SMS or Facebook Messenger to send text messages, and they respond with an eye-roll. "Seriously? We're just making dinner plans," they might say. They might shrug off the suggestion to use Tor Browser by responding that they have nothing to hide, or that the government can surely find anything it needs with its super-spy

23. https://theintercept.com/series/oil-and-water/.
24. https://theintercept.com/2014/07/09/under-surveillance/.

technology. These responses disregard the reality that we build security by working together as a community. A properly formulated threat model considers a person's entire social graph, or community. Maybe we feel that our own situation does not require any amount of anonymity, but another person we communicate with might not be in the same situation. Using anonymizing technologies can also provide a kind of herd immunity: the more people use anonymizing technologies, the more widely accepted their use becomes. Anonymity loves company. The more people there are who use anonymity tools like Tor, the less a single Tor user stands out.

We can imagine libraries as pharmacies that offer free anonymity-flu shots. Educating and enabling patrons to protect their anonymity can help build a healthier community of technology users, leaving fewer members exposed to risk. Given libraries' role in offering vital Internet services to individuals who are likely to be subject to surveillance in other aspects of their lives, like low-income people and youth, it makes perfect sense for libraries to take on the responsibility of establishing safe, surveillance-resistant environments for these populations to research and conduct their online business. Like flu shots that only vaccinate against certain strains of a virus, libraries can't promise to protect everyone in all situations; however, we can offer best practices and safer spaces, both in the physical and virtual realms.

ADVERSARIES

In order for librarians to better understand the unique threat models of our communities, we need to understand the adversaries that our communities face. An adversary in this case is anyone who seeks to de-anonymize a person, whether their intent is malicious or not. Adversaries can be anyone, from a well-resourced state actor to a single disgruntled Internet user to an advertising company sending beacons to a website visitor. We've sorted common adversaries into three categories—state actors, corporate actors, and individual actors—in order to explain their capabilities and provide some examples of their activities. However, as we've already noted, there is sometimes crossover among these three, and they can often help each other, even if only incidentally.

State threat actors. In 2013, Edward Snowden revealed that the National Security Agency, in concert with other U.S. intelligence agencies and its foreign partners, had the capacity to spy on the digital communications of every person in the United States, whether or not they were citizens or foreign nationals, and regardless of whether they'd been accused of a crime or not. We learned that the NSA partnered with telecom companies to collect and store vast quantities of Internet traffic as it flowed through fiber optics cables and traveled from phone to phone: this unsavory archive encompassed e-mails, social media posts and direct messages, text messages, call metadata, browsing history, and more. We also learned that these surveillance powers aren't limited to the NSA—federal and local law enforcement agencies alike have tremendous legal authority and an arsenal of tools at their disposal.

In many cases, citizens don't even know the extent to which law enforcement can monitor them, because the police don't—and won't—talk about their capabilities. Recently, a controversial policing tool called an IMSI catcher (often referred to by the brand name of the most common model, Stingray) has garnered media attention. An IMSI catcher masquerades as a cell tower. If you pass by it within a certain range, your phone assumes that it's a cell tower, and broadcasts your location and your phone's unique ID to this device. Furthermore, IMSI catchers can even listen to unencrypted calls in real time, or deliver malware to the device, or intercept and read unencrypted data transmitted from the phone. Police say they're using these to catch specific suspects, but the devices function by slurping up *all* cell phone traffic within their range. Even if the police only have a warrant to track a specific individual, once they have data for hundreds of people, there's nothing—technologically, at least—to stop them from using the data they've gathered to locate or track other individuals. Because your phone's service provider can connect the unique identity of your device to your personal identity, a Stingray allows the police to flag a person's whereabouts easily and efficiently. No one knows how broadly these devices have been adapted, though, because "as a condition for purchasing them, state and local police forces must sign strict non-disclosure agreements with the FBI, since the more information is made public about cell-site simulators, the more 'adversaries' will adapt to them."[25] The technology behind Stingrays is opaque, and activists and lawmakers alike do not fully understand their capabilities.[26] As with many de-anonymizing technologies, it's easy to argue in favor of the police having access to Stingrays. An advocate might propose their value in a situation like a search for a missing child. But the possibilities for the devices' misuse are equally broad: police can theoretically use them simply to view and track individuals as they go about their daily routines, isolating patterns they deem somehow suspicious and zeroing in on people who follow those routes. When we discuss state-sponsored surveillance, we might start to sound like tinfoil-hat paranoids, but it is a fact that the government has incredibly powerful technologies at its

---

25. https://www.economist.com/news/united-states/21689244-courts-take-aim
   -technology-beloved-countrys-police-forces-secretive.
26. https://techcrunch.com/2017/06/02/who-catches-the-imsi-catchers-researchers
   -demonstrate-stingray-detection-kit/.

disposal, and we've seen these new technologies used again and again in violation of our basic civil liberties.

Aside from technical surveillance apparatus, the government has a broad ability to subpoena records—so long as they exist. One of the most chilling recent examples involves the case against the "J20" protesters, a group of people arrested during Inauguration Day protests in January 2017. In order to build a case against these protesters, the Department of Justice (DOJ) issued a warrant to a web-hosting company called DreamHost, which hosts the website DisruptJ20.org that had aggregated information about the inauguration and the protests, as well as more general information about organizing actions and protests. The warrant requested all information stored on the website—databases, files, and logs of the IP addresses of 1.3 million individuals who had visited the site. Theoretically, the DOJ could merely have requested information about whether or not a handful of IP addresses associated with those protesters currently facing charges for felony rioting were stored in the logs. Instead, it opted to request everything. Whether you were a protester, a reporter looking for information about potential actions, a police officer trying to figure out what to prepare for, or just a curious Internet user, your information and identity as a potential anti-Trump resister is now in the government's hands. You may have thought that by not logging in to the website, or by using a fake name, you were protecting your identity. But the fundamental design of the Web and the broad surveillance powers of the federal government made that impossible; it's not inconceivable that all visitors to that site are now on some kind of list that prioritizes them for further monitoring.

In general, the government would rather you didn't stay anonymous. The presence of Tor Browser—the only web browser that can provide anonymity for its users—on individuals' computers is seen as a threat and potential evidence of wrongdoing by law enforcement. The NSA logs the IP addresses of people who visit the Tor website,[27] marking them as suspicious by default. When the accused leaker Reality Winner was interviewed by the FBI, she acknowledged that she had Tor Browser downloaded on her laptop, saying "[it] probably looks bad"[28] and defensively assuring the agent interviewing her that she had only used it once. In an NSA presentation released with the Snowden documents, an official describes the rationales for Tor's existence as "pseudo-legitimate" and hammers home the point that "bad people" use the service.[29] Similarly, law enforcement services view encrypted mail, messaging, and devices as a threat, and refer to their decreasing ability to monitor communications as consumers opt to use encrypted technologies as "going dark." A 2016 bill proposed by senators Dianne Feinstein and Richard Burr[30] aimed to ban end-to-end encryption in order to make more information—encrypted data on phones, for instance—accessible to law enforcement. Although the bill failed, some legislators continue to perceive encryption as suspicious, as though an individual's desire to protect her data from attackers implies that she has something to hide. In October 2017, Deputy Attorney General Rod Rosenstein asserted in a speech that "encrypted communications that cannot be intercepted and locked devices that cannot be opened are law-free zones that permit criminals and terrorists to operate without detection by police and

---

27. https://motherboard.vice.com/en_us/article/d73yd7/how-the-nsa-targets-tor-users.

28. https://www.documentcloud.org/documents/4334950-Reality-Winner-Interrogation
     -Transcript.html.

29. https://www.theguardian.com/world/2013/oct/04/nsa-gchq-attack-tor-network
     -encryption.

30. https://techcrunch.com/2016/04/13/burr-feinstein-encryption-bill-is-officially
     -here-in-all-its-scary-glory/.

without accountability by judges and juries." He argued instead for "responsible encryption" that would render all devices and data somehow accessible to law enforcement.[31] This attitude echoes the stances of some repressive governments, like those in Turkey and Iran, which attempt to prevent the use of Tor Browser[32] and encrypted text apps like Signal or WhatsApp through both legislation and technical exploits. If legislators continue to portray encryption and anonymous communication as harmful and pass bills regulating their use, we could find ourselves in a situation where all of our data can be monitored by law enforcement. At this time, though, encryption's increasing ubiquity—for instance, all iPhones are encrypted by default—may mean that its opponents will face an uphill battle.

Corporate powers. When we do privacy and anonymity trainings, we tell our audiences to open their phones and look at how many apps they have that automatically track their location. People are almost always taken aback. The Major League Baseball app tracks me? The app for every airline I've ever used—airlines which require me to download their app to get flight status updates—gathers information about my location? My streaming music app has access to my contacts? Why do all these companies need to know where I go and what I do?

Data about you—your location, your interests, your age and sexual preference and favorite movie, and the frequency with which you order certain products from certain websites—is a commodity. In fact, this data is the business model of the Internet. Services like Facebook and Gmail are free because of the value they accrue from collecting your personal data. They resist anonymizing you because it costs them financially. An entire industry of data brokers exists to aggregate and sell

31. https://www.lawfareblog.com/deputy-attorney-general-rod-rosenstein-remarks-encryption.
32. https://motherboard.vice.com/en_us/article/ae3am5/iran-is-trying-to-block-tor.

profiles of individuals from bits of data gleaned from apps, location trackers, cookies, sales data, widgets, and so on. Every time you use an app, you send nuggets of information about yourself out through multiple channels, for others' profit. Every website or service that uses advertising shares information about you with countless third parties in order to attract their advertising dollars, and those advertisers in turn collect even more information about you, your likes and preferences, the sites that you visit, how much time you spend on them, and more. The controversy over Cambridge Analytica's use of Facebook data to attempt to influence election results has shed light on this practice for many, but these practices have existed for years and are ingrained in how businesses operate on the Internet today.

In 2012, the journalist Charles Duhigg interviewed Target employees about how they tracked consumer shopping habits, linking every interaction a customer had with the store (purchases, coupon use, customer service inquiries) to a unique ID, and purchasing additional information from third-party data vendors.[33] The store analyzed this data alongside records of the items that customers bought in order to identify patterns in their lives and send them targeted ads: someone who bought several bathing suits in the spring would receive a coupon for sunscreen in July. Duhigg tells an anecdote of an infuriated father in Minnesota who went on a tirade to his local Target store manager about how inappropriate he found it that his household kept receiving coupons for maternity clothes and baby items—addressed to his teenage daughter.

> The manager apologized and then called a few days later to apologize again.

---

33. https://www.nytimes.com/2012/02/19/magazine/shopping-habits.html.

> On the phone, though, the father was somewhat abashed. "I had
> a talk with my daughter," he said. "It turns out there's been some
> activities in my house I haven't been completely aware of. She's due
> in August. I owe you an apology."

Target knew more about the family than they knew about each other.

Many corporate entities behave the way Target does, collecting huge amounts of information, often without our knowledge or explicit consent. Consider Facebook: we know that they collect the information that we directly give them, like our status updates and pictures. But they also collect lots of other information through the use of cookies (a small piece of identifiable data), which can be fed into an algorithm and used to sell us products or discriminate against us. Data collection is big business, which is why the tech giants Google, Amazon, Microsoft, Facebook, and Apple are worth a combined $3 trillion.[34] These companies make it convenient and desirable for us to surrender information, de-incentivizing privacy. Don't want to get up from the couch to change the music? Keep a "smart speaker" with a microphone on in your home at all times, listening. Want to visit an amusement park? Give Six Flags or Disney your fingerprint for entry. Interested in your family history? Send your DNA to a company that might share that information with law enforcement or insurance companies. Do you really want to trust all of these companies to act ethically, in your best interest—surely not in the interest of their own profitability—and to secure this data so it doesn't leak out? If our mission in writing this book was to catalog all of the recent examples of corporate data malfeasance and misuse, you'd be holding a much fatter volume.

---

34. https://motherboard.vice.com/en_us/article/mbxndq/one-month-without-big-five
   -microsoft-google-facebook-apple-amazon.

Not only are corporations amassing our data, but they generally want to stay on the government's good side. The NSA's mass surveillance project would be impossible without certain telecom and software companies' willing collaboration. When you entrust library data to a vendor's cloud service, consider whether a company would rather put money into fighting a subpoena for your patrons' data or would prefer to avoid the cost and hassle of a legal battle and just let Immigration and Customs Enforcement or the FBI walk in and view the contents of its servers. Unlike the government, corporate entities are not required to comply with the privacy protections outlined in the Fourth Amendment; instead, a legal theory called the third party doctrine says that when you share your personal data with a so-called "third party," you have "no reasonable expectation of privacy."[35] While there have been some important recent court victories[36] limiting how much the U.S. government can exploit this privacy loophole, along with the expansive privacy protections in the European Union's General Data Protection Regulation (GDPR) that rein in global corporate data collection, digital capitalists still rely on data for their bottom lines. Few companies have a great track record here, and some of the most powerful ones—Amazon, Facebook, Google—are responsible for normalizing the sharing of our personal data.

Human adversaries. A much more nebulous adversary emerges closest to home. Overbearing parents, abusive ex-partners, and trans-phobic teachers can all use private information against vulnerable targets. A search for "keylogger," a type of spyware that silently tracks everything a user types into their computer, pulls up websites that promise purchasers the ability to catch cheating spouses and make sure their kid "stays

---

35. https://en.wikipedia.org/wiki/Third-party_doctrine.
36. https://epic.org/amicus/location/carpenter/.

safe" online. Imagine a person in an abusive relationship searching for resources about domestic violence--only to have everything they do on their computer sent directly to the partner they're trying to escape. Imagine if the queer teen we described earlier had their pseudonymous blog exposed and linked to their real name by a snooping family member.

The ready availability of parent-controlled spyware and school surveillance technology means that individual adversaries can be everywhere, and what's worse, they often know their targets personally, making it especially challenging for a target to protect themselves. In some cases, adversaries who *don't* know their targets use these same tools—as well as the plethora of personal information that people inadvertently make available online—to dox them. Certain kinds of online activities—especially activism by women, queer and trans people, and people of color—may provoke doxing, but the nature of the Internet today makes these threats unpredictable. No one can determine when a certain social media post will go viral, prompting irate 4chan users or conspiracy theorists to harass a specific person. The family of one of the victims of the Sandy Hook mass killing has had to move seven times, because each time they moved, trolls who believe that the shooting was a hoax doxed them and published their address online.[37]

Now that we've overwhelmed you with terrifying examples that illustrate how powerful companies, fringe nut-cases, and various arms of law enforcement exploit your data, we want to reassure you that plenty of resources and organizations have made protecting anonymity and

---

37. https://www.nytimes.com/2018/07/31/us/politics/alex-jones-defamation-suit-sandy-hook.html.

Internet freedom a priority. Some groups address these threats from a policy orientation: Electronic Frontier Foundation and the American Civil Liberties Union litigate cases where they see governmental and corporate overreach, and they rally supporters to agitate for better legal protections for encryption, privacy, and net neutrality. These and similar organizations have also created educational materials around privacy and surveillance (see the "Resources" section at the end of this book for more examples). Some organizations, like Access Now and Crash Override Network, provide consulting services to at-risk populations and individuals. Still others focus on developing tools that help people navigate the Internet more securely: the Freedom of the Press Foundation, for example, developed SecureDrop; and the Guardian Project has created several useful apps, including ObscuraCam—a camera application that allows a user to strip metadata from a photo and blur out or pixelate the faces of bystanders that she doesn't want depicted in the image—and Orbot, a mobile version of Tor for Android devices.

Although these may seem like minor interventions in the digital landscape, these small victories can add up, and lead to wider acceptance of what once might have seemed like fringe technologies. For example, increased awareness of encryption—which is promoted by many of these groups—has led some apps, including Facebook Messenger and WhatsApp, to implement open-source encryption protocols, allowing the public to enable encryption in their messaging conversations, and to audit the technology used to encrypt these conversations. On a more basic level, the number of groups working to advocate for anonymity online means that you're not alone, and that—to put it simply—plenty of people who know a lot about computers have either thought through the concerns you might have or, if they haven't, will be interested in considering your use case from ethical, policy, or technological perspectives.

In our experience, many technologists who work in this sphere appreciate the chance to investigate the challenges posed by a situation they haven't encountered before.

Finally, Library Freedom Project (LFP), a small but mighty organization run by one of this book's authors, is dedicated to the protection and promotion of privacy in libraries. LFP teaches librarians about policy, rights, and technology in order to help libraries facilitate more privacy and anonymity in our library spaces and communities.

ANONYMITY IN LIBRARIES

LIBRARIANS FIGHT BACK

Libraries have long recognized that intellectual freedom can't exist without privacy. Our commitment to these values appears again and again in our policies. A key ALA document, the Code of Ethics,[38] holds that "we do not advance private interests at the expense of library users, colleagues, or our employing institutions." Efforts to minimize the reach that corporations have into our patrons' lives fit squarely into this commitment. The ALA's Freedom to Read Statement[39] further posits that if your access to certain materials is constrained—as it might be if you feel that what you read is being monitored—you miss out on a world of new ideas. Librarians have historically interpreted our professional commitment to privacy to mean that we should protect

38. http://www.ala.org/advocacy/sites/ala.org.advocacy/files/content/
    proethics/codeofethics/Code%20of%20Ethics%20of%20the%20
    American%20Library%20Association.pdf.
39. http://www.ala.org/advocacy/intfreedom/freedomreadstatement.

the checkout histories of patrons from disclosure. Nowadays, however, libraries deal with patron data in much greater quantities. We no longer simply hold checkout histories or patron account records: we may now possess logs of computer and printer use, browser histories, records of the use of library databases and other digital resources, and evidence of patrons' physical presence in the library as logged on CCTV cameras.

Though anonymity is not often thought of as a "traditional library value," its necessity is becoming increasingly clear in this environment of massive data creation and collection and digital surveillance. If only four data points[40] are needed to de-anonymize me, then I can't have true intellectual freedom in any digital context unless the service or tool I am using has no information about my real identity. If we librarians want to live up to our values in the twenty-first century, we must make it possible for patrons to use our buildings and services *as anonymously as possible*, taking their individual threat models and adversaries into account. To do this, we must begin by assessing our current practices and services in order to understand how we collect and store identifying information about our patrons.

PROFESSIONAL VALUES IN PRACTICE

Privacy is a prerequisite for anonymity, and although libraries have ethical commitments to privacy, most libraries fall far short of this ideal in practice. It is impossible to use most libraries anonymously, or even privately, given the way that information is collected, stored, and shared. Librarians reading this text may find that fact alarming,

---

40. https://bits.blogs.nytimes.com/2015/01/29/with-a-few-bits-of-data-researchers
    -identify-anonymous-people/.

particularly because the popular understanding among many librarians is that libraries stopped keeping all patron records after the passage of the USA PATRIOT Act, and even fought a National Security Letter[41] for patron data. The good news is that professional dedication to privacy seem to be growing ever stronger, with efforts like the Data Privacy Project,[42] the San Jose Public Library's Virtual Privacy Lab,[43] and Library Freedom Project[44] popping up just in the last few years. But libraries still have many practical steps to take before they fall in line with the sentiments codified in our core documents. So where do we begin?

ANONYMITY AND PRIVACY INEQUALITIES

Before we can make significant pro-anonymity changes to our library spaces and practices, we need to think about threat modeling again. Not every person in our communities experiences the loss of privacy or the need for anonymity in the same way, and existing social inequities due to race, class, gender, and so on affect both the need for anonymity and the likelihood that a person will be able to achieve it. The activist Mariame Kaba urges those of us who think about privacy and anonymity to "focus on the low tech as opposed to the spectacular" forms of surveillance.[45] She recounts how the young black people she's worked with in Chicago talk about being followed around local businesses by shop-owners and routinely accosted on the street by police officers who

---

41. https://www.nytimes.com/2006/05/31/nyregion/31library.html.
42. https://dataprivacyproject.org/.
43. https://www.sjpl.org/privacy.
44. https://libraryfreedomproject.org/.
45. Talk given at the "Subverting Surveillance" conference at Barnard College, February 17, 2018.

know and recognize them; because they live in public housing projects, these youths' expectation of privacy even within their own homes differs from that of young people who grow up in neighborhoods with yards and fences.

Underscoring Kaba's point, at a March 2018 talk at the New Museum in New York, the Native American activist Madonna Thunder Hawk described how useful she found Facebook as an organizing and communications tool during the protests against the Dakota Access Pipeline. When asked if she felt concerned that the pipeline protesters' communications were being accessed by law enforcement or the private security firm that worked for the company building the pipeline, Thunder Hawk—a veteran of the American Indian Movement, one of many 1970s activist groups that was infiltrated by the FBI through its infamous COINTELPRO program—simply laughed. "We're always being monitored," she said. To her, the loss of privacy that Facebook represents, and the window into her life and activities it could provide, seem completely irrelevant in the face of her life experience as a subject of so many other kinds of surveillance.

An "unspectacular" loss of privacy also extends into the amount of information the government demands from certain categories of people. In her book *Automating Inequality*, the scholar Virginia Eubanks writes about how the surveillance of poor Americans extends beyond in-person encounters into the intimate details of people's lives. In many states, in order to access government benefits like housing and health care, applicants must provide the government with broad swaths of information that middle-class Americans would consider highly confidential: details about one's health history, family, past experience with addiction, and past run-ins with the law. Our professional commitment to patron privacy needs to reflect the unequal distribution of privacy that different races and classes experience, and to conceive of ways that our spaces can avoid amplifying the surveillance that many of our patrons face.

Librarians must understand that the very idea of anonymity might understandably be laughable to people living with these realities. The benefits of anonymizing technologies can't undo the effects of systemic racism and inequality. Therefore, we must consider how the loss of privacy is just one aspect of larger overarching systems of oppression, and situate our work protecting privacy and promoting anonymity within a greater anti-oppressive framework: one that is antiracist, antisexist, and class-conscious. From there, we can start to build library environments that reflect our professional commitments to privacy and freedom of information, and our respect for the lived realities of our community members. With regard to privacy, as with many other issues, we need to stay aware of the conditions in which our patrons live and to trust their own experiences of their lives, and then think about what resources we can mobilize to serve them.

PRIVACY POLICIES AND PROCEDURES: A STARTING POINT FOR ANONYMITY

Significant progress has been made to bring library values into line with library practices in the realm of policy best practices. Two efforts in particular stand out: the ALA Library Privacy Checklists,[46] created by the IFC Privacy Subcommittee and the LITA Patron Privacy Interest Group; and the Principles on User's Digital Privacy in Library, Publisher,

---

46. http://www.ala.org/advocacy/privacy/checklists.

and Software-Provided Systems[47] under the auspices of NISO (National Information Standards Organization). Both documents outline a set of best practices for library user privacy, including minimizing the amount of personally identifying information (PII) and protecting PII that libraries keep. They call for any PII stored by the library or its vendors to be anonymized and stored securely; for libraries and vendors to state clearly why they collect any of this information; to collect data only when they have a distinct purpose for doing so; and to educate the public on privacy protections. Overall, these documents demand that all third-party providers that libraries use for digital services follow the same core principles that respect a library user's freedom to read and research privately that we librarians ask of ourselves.

These documents can also help us apprehend the many ways that library service can de-anonymize our patrons. Popular integrated library systems, which store patron account and checkout data, routinely delete checkout information once the patrons return their materials. When we think about "library records," we typically mean these checkout records, and then we proudly declare that we've addressed library-related privacy issues. Those records, however, are hardly the only sensitive data generated through the use of library services. The moment a patron walks into the building, her movements may be tracked by CCTV cameras that feed either to library or municipal IT personnel, and possibly also to local law enforcement. Once inside, if the patron uses a library PC, the library card information which she uses to log on to the machine is likely stored in the authentication software. If she connects her mobile device to the library's Wi-Fi, the identifying information about her device is communicated to library IT, and possibly also logged. If she visits a

47. https://groups.niso.org/apps/group_public/download.php/16064/NISO%20Privacy%20Principles.pdf.

library database from her mobile device, her IP information is shared with that database; she may also be tracked by third parties that are collecting analytics for the database provider. The most popular library e-book platform, OverDrive, keeps a history of all of her checkouts of those materials, and shares that information with Amazon. When the patron visits the library's website, she may be tracked by a host of private companies (including Facebook and Twitter) using "share this" widgets, and she may be tracked by other third parties, including advertisers and analytics companies. What are these providers' data retention policies? How long do they keep the information, and who has access to it? How securely do they store this data? When it comes to digital resources in libraries, we haven't spent enough time asking and answering these questions. For instance, some libraries use the streaming service Kanopy to provide their patrons with access to an extensive collection of motion pictures. Many films on Kanopy are not available on other services like Netflix or Hulu, and it provides an option for patrons who don't wish to incur the cost of subscribing to one of those services. It's also relatively affordable for libraries as a way to license and serve this type of content. A quick glance at Kanopy's privacy policy, though, shows that it "may access, collect, monitor, and/or store" the location data for individual users, and that it "may share information about you with third-party business associates." Naturally, anonymity-seeking users can opt not to use the service, but one wonders whether librarians consider or debate providing access to this kind of user data when they begin working with a new third-party provider. By using the ALA Privacy Checklists and the NISO Principles, we can create standards for ourselves and for our vendors that enable more anonymous library usage.

ANONYMITY BASICS

We talked to a number of librarians who are starting to incorporate anonymity tools and practices into the services they offer their patrons, and we asked them what they'd suggest to other librarians who want to get started. Many noted that in order to get buy-in from other library staff and boards, a good first step is a succinct argument about why anonymity matters and how it connects to our professional values of open access, the freedom to read, and privacy. Even some people who work in libraries view a desire for anonymity online as tied intrinsically to an intent to do sinister things. Teaching our peers about the tools they can use and the extent to which their own data has spilled out into the hands of corporations, governments, and "people they may know" both prepares them to answer patrons' questions and demystifies the topic of anonymity. Also, librarians should remember what Mariame Kaba says about how privacy violations can take low-tech forms as well. Invite your colleagues to join you in looking around your library's public computer workstations and ask yourselves how the environment promotes or violates privacy, and how it would look if it allowed for anonymity. Here are some starting questions:

- Are there CCTV cameras pointed at any of the computers that show what's on screen?
- Can patrons easily see each other's screens?
- When library staff and security walk around the room, do they look over patrons' shoulders at the screens?

You should also think about the library's layout. Shannon O'Neill, currently an archivist at Barnard College and formerly a librarian at the Atlantic City Public Library in New Jersey, remembers that in her library branch, a police officer sat right at the entrance of the library, immediately adjacent to the reference desk. The officers who provided security in the library also patrolled the nearby neighborhoods—immediately communicating that anyone who came into the library was subject to surveillance—and many patrons reported that they'd had negative experiences with these same individual officers. For these patrons, it became impossible to have an anonymous browsing or researching experience in the library. Many of them were known to local law enforcement by name. O'Neill also remembers that the library situated the computer terminals in the middle of the room, with no privacy guards to prevent any passersby from snooping on other users' computers.

Like many libraries, the Atlantic City library also had an anti-pornography policy. The police officers would make rounds in the library, checking to make sure that patrons complied with this policy. Again, this quite literal surveillance constrained patrons' ability to research privately or anonymously; once an individual had been identified as a person who looked at "inappropriate" material, they then had a reputation that led to scrutiny of their computer usage.

As you think about these problems, consider what potential pro-privacy, pro-anonymity solutions might be available. For the situations described above, privacy guards on computer screens could protect patrons' privacy and prevent other patrons from being offended by what they see on each other's screens. Discouraging law enforcement officers from monitoring users and moving officers away from prominent positions in the library creates a more welcoming environment. Relocating computers to a more private area conveys that the library does not wish to judge or monitor patrons' computer use. Likewise, anonymous guest passes can facilitate slightly more identity-safe computer use (the patron is still not anonymous to Google or whatever services she logs in to, but there will be no record in the library's authentication software that one particular person used that particular computer). Obviously, these steps require institutional buy-in, but they are relatively easy and inexpensive places to begin. They also don't make big demands on staff, technology, or training. While none of these alterations alone will guarantee anonymity, they can help make patrons conditionally anonymous—for example, anonymous to the patron sitting right next to them. These small steps matter.

Given the high interest in online privacy, which has been sparked in part by the backlash against the corporate use of personal data uncovered in the Facebook-Cambridge Analytica controversy, our present moment is a perfect time to start these conversations. Library staff and patrons who might not previously have regarded anonymity as a high priority may come to change their minds as they realize the extent to which they've allowed corporations to peer into their private lives. Taking steps to protect data which tells so much about ourselves is neither outrageous nor radical.

While interest in anonymity is growing—some examples include the post-2016 election boom in Cryptoparties,[48] where people learn how to protect their identities online; and the 2018 #deletefacebook movement after the Cambridge Analytica scandal—the adoption of anonymizing practices is another story. Most libraries that take active measures to protect their patrons' identities do so in small (albeit important) ways, like those we discussed above, including privacy screens and anonymous guest passes. Librarians interested in promoting anonymity and privacy in the library may find unique challenges, since it can be difficult to explain to some patrons why these issues matter. Melissa Morrone of

---

48. https://www.npr.org/sections/alltechconsidered/2017/02/06/513705825/cryptoparties
-teach-attendees-how-to-stay-anonymous-online.

the Brooklyn Public Library says that many of her patrons treat any online form "like it's something at the doctor's office," readily volunteering their private information without a second thought about why the website is asking for certain information, who might be able to see it, and how it might be exploited. This reflects both a lack of awareness of Internet privacy, and the issue of privacy's inequitable availability to different people in society. The more librarians serve as providers of vital social services—in O'Neill's library, for example, workers at city agencies directed benefits applicants to fill out food stamps applications at the public library—the more they come into contact with people who, because of their precarious place in society, are constantly in the position of providing intimate details about their lives to the state. These patrons come to the library ready to relinquish their anonymity, and consequently force librarians to reflect on what we can do institutionally to ensure their individual safety.

At the same time, James Hutter of the Port Washington Public Library in New York points out that anonymity and online surveillance are "not a foreign concept to our patrons anymore. [The Equifax hack] was something people were well aware of, but they didn't understand the technical side of it, or how their personal info gets out there. They came to us with a lot of questions about that." To help such patrons, librarians should prepare answers and instructions about how to protect individuals' identities online. Other librarians told us that once they started posting privacy tips around the library, like signs near the computer terminals explaining how to use the Tor browser and ad-blockers, they received more requests for assistance and information.

ANONYMITY TECH

Librarians who want to help patrons to search and browse anonymously can start with some easy-to-use privacy technologies. Installing these tools on library computers helps start crucial conversations about anonymity, and builds patrons' trust in unfamiliar technologies. Remember, not all privacy technologies are anonymizing, but they can nevertheless provide some protection against certain adversaries or exploits. The web browsers on public computers are a great starting point. Choose either Firefox or Chrome as the default browser, and encourage patrons to use "private browsing/incognito mode." Private browsing/incognito mode has limited utility; it prevents the browser from saving information about your activity on the computer you're using, but it does not conceal your identity from websites you visit. Nevertheless, it is an easy way to create a pro-privacy habit among patrons and also dispel myths about what private browsing actually does and doesn't do.

We also recommend installing a couple of free, trusted browser extensions that offer some privacy features:

- Privacy Badger, which detects cookies and other trackers and prevents them from learning about user activity (helping you to be a little more anonymous from advertisers)
- HTTPS Everywhere, which forces websites with security certificates to always use HTTPS (thus preventing anyone snooping on Internet traffic from learning anything about you through unencrypted data)

Neither of these extensions significantly affects browsers' performance; although Privacy Badger sometimes blocks plug-ins and other relevant content, a user can disable it easily. To foster patrons' understanding, you can create signage that explains these tools and their utility around the computer area.

Deep Freeze—or a trusted Deep Freeze alternative—is a software application which ensures that the computer system restores between each user and does not save user history, passwords that a patron inadvertently saved, and so on. This type of protection is absolutely essential, and is critical for preserving anonymity between each patron computer session.

The LibraryBox project, created by Jason Griffey of the University of Tennessee at Chattanooga, offers a novel method for accessing resources in a way that is free of de-anonymizing corporate control. LibraryBox is essentially a tiny server connected to a low-power router. It's not connected to the wider Internet, but anyone within the router's range can use a Wi-Fi-enabled device to access the content that is served to the local network. Libraries in areas with little or no Internet connectivity have used these systems to provide resources to their patrons; other libraries have set them up to promote works by local authors and creators. This kind of network is designed to be maximally accessible, so—in its current iteration—its traffic is not masked and is legible to network users. That said, a detached, locals-only network that's entirely controlled and monitored by an individual library has promise as an anonymizing technology insofar as it exists outside of the corporately controlled Internet. In an emergency that shuts off access to the larger Internet—whether human-made, like a political crackdown, or environmental, like a hurricane that severs connection to fiber optic cables—a hyper-local network like this can allow a library to maintain online materials for patrons. With additional security safeguards, this kind of network could potentially serve as a "banned book" repository or a (geographically) local communication hub that does not require its users to pay mobile service providers and does not require identifying information.

Libraries that are serious about providing anonymity as a service to patrons should consider using Tor, one of the best ways to browse the Internet anonymously. Tor is free software and an open network that helps its users stay safe from surveillance and censorship. One of this book's authors works with the Tor Project on outreach and community-building, including helping librarians set up Tor Browser on library PCs, running Tor relays from library networks, and teaching about Tor in library computer classes. On a more conceptual level, explaining Tor to patrons can also help them understand how the infrastructure of the Internet works and how many private entities interact with Internet traffic.

Tor Browser is the most common and simplest way of using Tor. The browser is a patched version of the Mozilla Firefox browser that routes a user's traffic through the Tor network. The Tor network randomly assigns three relays, and a layer of encryption between each relay prevents anyone from observing the websites the user is visiting or where in the world she is coming from. These relays are just computers that are configured to forward traffic. Relays are operated by volunteers all over the world who donate bandwidth, server space, and time to help make the Tor network stronger and more secure. The idea of a volunteer-run computer network that promises privacy might provoke some raised eyebrows, but rest assured, the Tor network is designed to put as little trust in these relays as possible.

When a user connects to Tor Browser and types in the website she wants to visit, the network randomly assigns a relay circuit. The first relay in the circuit receives the traffic and decrypts the first layer, which tells it what the second relay in the circuit is. This means that the first relay—known as the guard—knows the real IP information of the user, and the second relay in the circuit. Likewise, the second relay knows its origin—the first relay—and decrypts a layer to learn the location of the third relay. The third and final relay—known as the exit—decrypts the final layer to reach the user's destination website. This means that no single relay will know both the originating IP address and the destination website. The destination website will think that the Tor user is coming from the IP address associated with the exit relay. With every new web domain the user visits, she'll get a new circuit, meaning that each website thinks that she's a totally different person. This helps prevent websites from knowing what other sites she's visiting.

Tor Browser does more than just hide your location information. It also prevents different kinds of third-party tracking, leaves no trace of your activity on your computer, and prevents your ISP (Internet service provider) and anyone else who is observing your traffic from knowing the websites you visit. Websites don't know anything about you unless you log in or enter information about yourself. Even when you do log in, Tor has other beneficial privacy properties. For example, Facebook still knows who you are over Tor, but Facebook won't know where in the world you're coming from or other websites you're visiting.

Tor Browser is free to download from torproject.org, and can be used in much the same way as a "vanilla" browser to visit websites. It has some usability limitations, like occasional slowness, some websites serving "captchas" to users, and every once in a while, a site being completely blocked over Tor. This happens because the volume of traffic coming from a single IP on the Tor network can be perceived by system administrators as unusually high, making Tor traffic look suspicious and prompting additional security checks. However, for most web browsing, Tor will function in much the same way as a regular old browser. Better usability has also become a priority for Tor developers.

Many libraries now offer Tor Browser as an option on public desktop computers. Tor Browser can be installed alongside other, more common web browsers, and it should not be made the default browser on any public computer lest it cause some confusion to the users. Signage that briefly explains what Tor Browser is, how it works, and why the library has chosen to install it on the computers can go a long way towards building understanding about Tor among library users. Library Freedom Project even has a printable poster exactly for this purpose.[49] By running Tor Browser on library PCs, libraries can provide an anonymous means of using the Internet in the safe and trusted space of the library. Widespread adoption of Tor Browser in libraries will help the public gain a better understanding of Tor, which can also serve to make anonymity more mainstream as a concept.

Tor's opponents often cite examples of the use of its services for genuinely harmful purposes. The very structure of Tor that allows activists to use it to avoid government surveillance and censorship means that no top-level administrators have control over, access to, or even knowledge of every website on their network, which means that some illegal and harmful content can appear on those sites. In 2017, following the Charlottesville protests and the murder of Heather Heyer by a man who self-identified as "alt-right," Internet service providers like GoDaddy, Google, and CloudFlare removed the domain of the neo-Nazi news site, the Daily Stormer. The site promptly moved to an onion service, a website that is only accessible via Tor. The Tor Project responded with a blog post calling the neo-Nazis "disgusting,"[50] but clarified that there was nothing that Tor could do to take down the site, given how onion services work. But there are also many examples of onion services used

---

49. https://libraryfreedomproject.org/wp-content/uploads/2016/10/Tor-Poster-1.png.
50. https://blog.torproject.org/tor-project-defends-human-rights-racists-oppose.

for good purposes, some of which we discussed earlier (like Sci-Hub and SecureDrop), and others which we'll describe below in detail. Ultimately, the more people who choose to use Tor and the more services that rely on it, the lower the overall percentage of pernicious content and malevolent users will be, and more people will have freedom and privacy online: a win-win situation.

ANONYMITY LITERACY

Installing software is a great passive way to introduce patrons to anonymity technology, but what about a more active approach? A massive public education effort around anonymity, privacy, surveillance, and the Internet would be a game-changer for the public consciousness. Evidence shows that our communities want to see this happen. The 2015 Pew study "Libraries at the Crossroads"[51] found that 76 percent of respondents said that libraries should "definitely" offer programs to teach people how to protect their privacy and security online. If every library offered one class on understanding and controlling your data trail, this knowledge could become mainstream. Since the inception of Library Freedom Project, libraries across the United States, Canada, and the United Kingdom have learned how to teach privacy classes for their communities. The Data Privacy Project has done the same for the New York City metropolitan area. Electronic Frontier Foundation maintains multiple resources[52] for teaching yourself and others about anonymity and privacy.[53] The time has never been better for offering these classes in libraries. Here are some ways to get started:

---

51. http://www.pewinternet.org/2015/09/15/libraries-at-the-crossroads/.
52. https://ssd.eff.org/.
53. https://sec.eff.org.

- Connect with Electronic Frontier Foundation (EFF)[54] or your local ACLU affiliate.[55] Tell them you're a librarian who is interested in teaching online anonymity to your community, and ask if they have any tips or advice. Ask your ACLU affiliate if they could send a knowledgeable activist or lawyer to speak for a few minutes at this program. Even if that person doesn't actually know much about anonymity, having an ACLU representative speak about the right to privacy is a powerful way to kick off an otherwise more technically focused program.

- Find out if any groups in your community offer cryptoparties.[56] Cryptoparty is a grassroots global initiative to teach privacy and anonymity tools. In many cities, local privacy activists host these events, and they might be willing to come and teach at your library, or help you teach a class yourself. Here are some ideas for classes:
    - Introduction to privacy and anonymity
    - Following the path your data takes through the Internet
    - Who owns your data?
    - Incorporating anonymity tools into other introductory computer classes

- Organize a staff training event with Library Freedom Project.[57]

- Check out the resources on the ALA's Choose Privacy Week website.[58]

- Run a week-long or month-long Data Detox challenge in your library using Tactical Tech's Data Detox Kit.[59] The Data Detox

---

54. eff.org.
55. https://www.aclu.org/about/affiliates.
56. https://www.cryptoparty.in/.
57. libraryfreedomproject.org.
58. https://chooseprivacyeveryday.org/.
59. https://datadetox.myshadow.org/en/detox.

Kit is an eight-day program for taking control of your digital life. Through short daily exercises—for example, doing a reverse image search on a picture that a person uses as a profile picture in order to see how many places it's duplicated online beyond the site where she originally posted it—the kit helps a user think about her data trail, clean up places where data leaks, and better manage her online identity in the future.

Providing information about privacy and anonymity also builds trust within your patron community. The New Hampshire librarian Chuck McAndrew told a story that demonstrates how professional development among librarians, alongside awareness-raising campaigns on digital privacy and anonymity, can make a tangible difference for a patron:

> I had a man come in and talk to me at my library because he was very worried about the fact that he's transgender becoming public knowledge, but he wanted to go online and interact with other people in his same situation for support, resources, [and to feel] like he's not alone. I was able to show him some ways to protect his anonymity online so he could go out and interact with other people. Not everyone who gets involved with trans communities online has good intentions; some people are there to dox them. All of the work our library had done up to that point is why he came to us: we had already demonstrated that our library cared about these issues, we were already helping people, we had already identified ourselves as a privacy-protective space, and it gave him the confidence to come and talk to me, which was a huge risk for him.

FOR THE FUTURE

FRANKLY, THE FUTURE OF THE INTERNET LOOKS bleak, when viewed from the standpoint of privacy and anonymity. Our Internet activity is increasingly confined to a handful of services owned by a small number of metastasizing private companies. Governments and corporations have closed in on near-total control of the Internet, all while we welcome more shiny, connected gadgets into our lives in the form of Apple Watches, Amazon Echos, Samsung so-called Smart TVs, and a whole menagerie of connected baby monitors, refrigerators, children's toys, fitness trackers, and other gewgaws with chips in them. We must take immediate, substantial steps to change what services we use and how we use them, so we may salvage our collective connected future and the democratic potential of the Web. In libraries, we can grant our communities the ability to access the Internet in a way that gives them back some control over their data by teaching anonymity and offering anonymity services. In order to do this properly, we need to make significant changes encompassing trainings, service development, program offerings, reconfiguring of library spaces, and critically rethinking current practices.

WHAT DOES ANONYMITY LOOK LIKE IN THE LIBRARY OF THE FUTURE?

It may feel daunting to tackle a problem this massive, especially when the real solutions have to be long-term political ones involving lawmakers and community leaders. But we can only think about offering anonymity from a harm-reduction framework. We have limited interactions with our patrons; we cannot guarantee them full anonymity no matter what we teach them; and we recognize that forces outside of our control demand their information and identities in both the lawful and illicit ways that we've outlined above. We can, however, build awareness and teach techniques that minimize the risks that our patrons face from adversaries, and create communities where patrons protect each other, and where we work together to demand that people in power—whether on the library board, in the government, or at the companies that provide us with services—do better.

ADVOCACY

In the early days of the Snowden revelations, many librarians joked about how all of a sudden, the media were breathlessly covering a new, secret source of information: metadata. "We've been trying to get people to think about metadata for years!" a friend told one of the authors. Librarians understand the power of systems, data, cataloging, and labeling because we think about these issues every day. We understand that metadata exists for identification purposes, so metadata collected about our communications and browsing habits uniquely link us back to ourselves. Obfuscating or deleting metadata is one way to achieve anonymity under certain circumstances. And metadata is just one example of how librarians have a special understanding of the power of information. This understanding—coupled with our professional ethical commitments, and our relationship with the public—positions us to serve as advocates for political and regulatory solutions to threats to anonymity in our communities. Librarians (and our professional bodies) must partner with organizations like Electronic Frontier Foundation and the ACLU to advocate for legislative solutions to problems like the collection of metadata and more.

Recently, members of the Society of American Archivists (SAA) used advocacy as a tool to protect identifying information. A group of practitioners conducted a research and education campaign around the use of body-worn cameras in local police forces. As the use of body cameras expanded in the mid-2010s (in no small part due to the Black Lives Matter movement's demand for police accountability), archivists found problems in the ways police handled the footage. This footage is often inaccessible to the public, despite its putative purpose of allowing the public insight into police activities. Police departments across America have wildly inconsistent storage practices and retention policies for this footage which, because it captures countless interactions police have with civilians, has myriad associated privacy concerns. Many archivists recognized these as issues deeply relevant to their expertise in records management, providing public access to information, digital preservation, and ethics. Consequently, the SAA now has an official position on police camera footage as a public record, stating that the organization has "a vested interest in developing and advocating for comprehensive policies to govern these records in the interest of serving the public good and affirming the importance of Black Lives."[60] Other professional organizations within the LIS field can similarly think about where their interests and expertise can bolster advocacy efforts in the realm of privacy and anonymity.

EDUCATION

Libraries have the unique ability to offer free education to our communities through public programs. Earlier in this book, we listed some options for library programming, like classes on using privacy technologies, best practices for using social networking sites, and cryptoparties where patrons can bring their own devices and chat with experts about how to better lock down their data. Libraries can also host town halls or public forums that discuss surveillance from a policy and civil rights perspective. Experts from advocacy organizations are often thrilled to be invited to participate in panels like these because they recognize the role that librarians play in their communities and in the broader fight for privacy rights; as one of our favorite ACLU lawyers told us, the people she likes to work with most are "librarians, nuns, and kids with braces." Education can happen outside of a traditional program environment, too. In some cities, activists offer walking tours that teach attendees about the local surveillance infrastructure that is "hidden in plain sight." This kind of activity would be a great event for a library to sponsor and a way to connect with the physical space and community outside the library's walls.

---

60. https://www2.archivists.org/statements/issue-brief-police-mobile-camera-footage-as-a-public-record.

SPACE

How can a library's space be reconfigured to allow for anonymity? Start by thinking about how the public computers are positioned. Is there any space where public PCs can be used without their screens being seen by others? You should make computer terminals as private as possible with privacy screens, and place them away from heavily trafficked areas so patrons won't feel someone is watching them use the Internet. Limit the use of CCTV and be aware of who retains the footage and how: for instance, would a third-party security company make footage available to police or Immigration and Customs Enforcement without asking the library? Think about the threat model of your patrons as you walk through the library space, and note any areas where library can improve.

TECHNOLOGY

Technology is both the biggest impediment to anonymity and also the greatest opportunity for granting anonymity within our library spaces. A privacy-focused library would make use of the following technological tools.

More with Tor: onion services. We've already introduced you to Tor Browser and its benefits; we think that Tor Browser should be installed on all the computers in any library. But there are ways to go even further with Tor beyond this simple installation. We've explained some of the use cases for Tor onion services, which are websites and other services that are only accessible over Tor. Because of onion services, Tor isn't just for browsing anonymously. The Tor network can also be used to communicate, share, and publish with a higher degree of privacy and security, including publishing websites. Websites configured using Tor end in the top-level domain ".onion." There are many uses for onion services, some that are more everyday and mundane than you might think. The largest onion service on the Internet is actually Facebook, which runs an onion service for users to access over Tor Browser: https://www.facebookcorewwwi.onion/ (but please note that if you're not using Tor Browser, that link won't open). Onion services provide privacy protection for both the user and the web server; when you run an onion site, no one knows where in the world you're really operating that site from, or who you are. Onion services protect the user both by requiring Tor Browser to access the site, and also by providing a similar set of privacy protections as HTTPS—confidentiality, authenticity of the site, and data integrity—without having to trust a private company to provide a security certificate. Onion services have both privacy and anti-censorship properties. The latter is why having an onion service appeals to a site like Facebook: they want their users in countries with censored or restricted Internet to be able to access Facebook. There are many examples of onion services being used in the public interest: the *New York Times*[61] and other news organizations have started spinning up their own onions, and the academic search engine Sci-Hub maintains an onion for when its regular website gets taken offline by copyright-enforcing global authorities. SecureDrop,[62] the open-source whistle-blower submission we discussed earlier, uses Tor onion services to protect whistle-blowers' anonymity. Do you want to share documents securely with friends, family, or your accountant? Use OnionShare,[63] a free tool that uses onion services to allow for secure and anonymous file-sharing.

---

61. https://open.nytimes.com/https-open-nytimes-com-the-new-york-times-as-a
   -tor-onion-service-e0d0b67b7482.
62. https://securedrop.org.
63. https://onionshare.org/.

Libraries could encourage anonymity by setting up an onion site to mirror their library websites. They can promote the use of onion services, like the examples we've given, or even set up their own SecureDrop instance for anonymous feedback related to things like local governance. Instructions for setting up SecureDrop, as well as other tips for safely leaking documents, are on the SecureDrop website.

Tor relays in libraries. In 2015, Library Freedom Project worked with the Lebanon Public Libraries (in New Hampshire) to set up a Tor relay on the library's network. Tor relays are the backbone of the Tor network, and are run by volunteers all over the world. Relays provide network strength and speed for the two million daily Tor users. Shortly after we set up this relay in New Hampshire, the library was contacted by local law enforcement—who had themselves been contacted by the Department of Homeland Security—asking the library to shut down the relay. A flood of local community protests and national media support got the relay turned back on quickly, but it showed just how much our government agencies feel threatened by the exercise of our basic civil right to freedom of speech. To us, it was a powerful testament to the necessity of running Tor relays in libraries, and something that more libraries should adopt if we truly want to take a stand for anonymity.

More Tor relays make the Tor network fast and stable. While it takes a reasonable amount of technical skill, many people who've started running relays have been surprised at how simple it actually is. Though we shared an example of law enforcement trying to interfere with relay operation, it is not illegal to run a relay, and most relay operators will never get hassled by law enforcement. Libraries are especially well-positioned to run relays because we already provide public Internet access, and so are shielded from some of the risks that an individual might face. Moreover, running a relay fits into our ethical commitments to intellectual freedom and privacy. By running a relay, we're helping people all over the world access the Internet more anonymously.

If your library wants to run a Tor relay, Library Freedom Project[64] will help you. For information about how to run a relay and relay operator best practices, visit the Tor Relay Guide.[65]

Tails as a service in libraries. It can be overwhelming to think about all the ways our data is leaked, collected, stored, and exploited. Making piecemeal changes to our behavior to maximize our anonymity can discourage even the most dedicated activist who needs it the most. Thankfully, a collective of developers have considered this problem and created an all-in-one anonymity solution called Tails. Tails stands for "The Amnesiac Incognito Live System," and its name tells you much about what it does. It's a live operating system, meaning that it can be installed on a flash drive and then booted into directly without making any permanent change to the computer it's running on, or interfering with the operating system installed on that computer. It is amnesiac in the sense that when the system is shut down and the Tails drive is removed, there is no trace of the user's activity on that computer (or on that flash drive, unless she explicitly configures it to persistently store some information). It is incognito because it routes all of its applications over the Tor network, giving the same location privacy properties of Tor Browser to the entire operating system. Tails is built from GNU/Linux Debian, so GNU/Linux users will find the interface and applications somewhat familiar, but Tails is also simple enough for most computer users to learn and understand. Installation requires a flash drive of at least 4 MB, a little bit of time, and the Tails ISO file downloaded from tails.boum.org, which comes with an easy-to-use installation wizard. It's also a pretty fun and exciting

---

64. libraryfreedomproject.org.
65. https://trac.torproject.org/projects/tor/wiki/TorRelayGuide.

piece of software. Who doesn't want to carry around a flash drive with a super-secret, ultra-anonymous operating system on it? Using Tails is cool.

PROFESSIONAL DEVELOPMENT

These days, professional development opportunities organized around anonymity and privacy abound. Here are some of our favorites:

Library Freedom Institute
https://libraryfreedomproject.org/lfi

Library Freedom Institute (LFI) is a four- to six-month program from Library Freedom Project that was born out of the demand for LFP's successful shorter privacy trainings. Funded by the Institute of Museum and Library Services (IMLS), LFI trains participants in practical privacy and anonymity strategies and skills through readings, webinars, class discussion, and assignments. It's totally free, and mostly online, with one in-person component. Application information for upcoming LFI rounds can be found at libraryfreedomproject.org/lfi.

Data & Society Trainings with METRO and Brooklyn Public Library
https://datasociety.net/initiatives/privacy/digital-privacy-data-literacy/

Another set of IMLS-funded initiatives are the Data & Society trainings in New York City, in partnership with the Brooklyn Public Library, METRO (The Metropolitan New York Library Council), and the New America Foundation. These trainings focus on data and privacy literacy by providing in-person education and training to more than 600 information and library professionals in the New York metropolitan area, as well as online resources to librarians across the country.

Virtual Privacy Lab at the San Jose Public Library
https://www.sjpl.org/privacy

The Virtual Privacy Lab provides toolkits to learn about privacy topics and customize a privacy toolkit geared to your online needs. The toolkits include links, tips, and resources that empower users to customize their online identities.

Surveillance Self-Defense and the Security Education Companion from Electronic Frontier Foundation
https://www.eff.org

Two excellent resources from Electronic Frontier Foundation can be used for professional development and patron programming. One is Surveillance Self-Defense,[66] a set of guidelines, tips, and tools for safer online communications. The other is the Security Education Companion,[67] a free resource for digital security educators that provides curriculums, training advice, and other learning tools. You can use it to teach others, or teach yourself.

SECURITY

As we think about harm reduction, we must consider the role that police and security have in libraries. Earlier, we cited an example of a public library where the presence of police—who also patrolled the neighborhood outside the library—unnerved patrons, making it impossible for them to be anonymous in the library and to conduct their business there without feeling watched. The same feeling of apprehension upon

---

66. https://ssd.eff.org/.
67. https://sec.eff.org/.

seeing security personnel probably applies to the patrons of other libraries around the country. That said, the professional literature about libraries and security often emphasizes how to build good relationships with local police or campus security, so that these forces hurry to the rescue every time an ostensibly shady character shows up in the library. A February 2018 article in *Library Journal* that encourages librarians to collaborate with law enforcement acknowledges that when librarians are trained to look for "suspicious" patron behavior, this "could lead to targeting of innocent patrons, such as homeless or mentally ill persons, or those fitting a particular racial profile."[68] We believe that librarians must feel safe in their workplaces. At the same time, we urge librarians to think about the damage that policing and surveillance do to many of the communities that we serve and to members of those communities' ability to exercise their "freedom to read," and to become aware of our own unconscious biases and the role those play in our perception of our own safety. Perhaps adding de-escalation and bystander intervention trainings in libraries and library schools could decrease our reliance on police and security guards as essential to library services.

Do no harm (or at least try not to). We've focused a lot on the concept of harm reduction as it relates to anonymity and privacy. One crucial aspect of this is to make sure that you don't over-promise. You should recognize the legal and technical limitations of what you can offer a user—most things are "best practices for most scenarios" and not a 100 percent guarantee of privacy or anonymity extending far into the future. The archives world had a sobering realization along these lines in the late 2000s,[69] when the U.S. Department of Justice subpoenaed

---

68. https://lj.libraryjournal.com/2018/02/public-services/guns-library-safety-security/#_.
69. https://www2.archivists.org/groups/oral-history-section/the-belfast-case-information -for-saa-members.

Boston College for items from the Belfast Project, a closed oral history collection held in its library. The interviewers who gathered oral histories for the project had promised the narrators—who spoke candidly about their involvement in serious crimes during the Troubles in Northern Ireland—that their accounts would be inaccessible at the library until their deaths. The subpoena and subsequent court case, in which judges found in favor of the Justice Department and required Boston College to hand over transcripts, proved that the donor agreements which Boston College had used (which had previously been a common donor agreement for many archives) could not stand up in court. Other interviewees contacted Boston College, terrified that the interviews they had provided—with the understanding that no one would hear them until they died—could be released to the British government and possibly put their lives in danger. The library ultimately deaccessioned the collection, returning the materials to the original donors. The fallout from this case has caused archivists to think seriously about what kinds of materials they can reasonably collect, what they can tell donors about the privacy and security of the collections they hold, and what might put individuals at risk once these materials enter an institutional context. Archives can no longer, in good faith, promise to keep a collection closed and now must, in effect, threat-model for their donors and for themselves. In a similar vein, everything that we advise others with regard to keeping their identities hidden will always just be a best effort and can never be a guarantee.

Keeping each other safe. Anonymity can seem like an individual choice, a personal rebellion against doing what society wants you to do, as though you have nothing to hide. When you think of anonymity and the Internet, you probably imagine a single person trying to slip by unnoticed, maybe a figure like Rami Malek's character in *Mr. Robot* who resists human contact. In truth, you can't be anonymous all by yourself. Here's a story about the beginnings of the Snowden saga that helps to show why the stereotype of some kind of "lone gunman" anonymous dude is fallacious.

When Edward Snowden decided he had an ethical obligation to release documents of the NSA's capacity to spy on all Americans' communications, he decided that filmmaker Laura Poitras, who made films about and had experienced government surveillance, would understand the data's implications and release it responsibly.[70] First, he needed to feel assured that he could contact Poitras securely. Rather than e-mailing Poitras directly, he e-mailed the technologist Micah Lee. Lee worked for Electronic Frontier Foundation and the Freedom of the Press Foundation, where Poitras was a board member. The then-anonymous Snowden asked Lee for the key that would allow him to send Poitras an encrypted e-mail; he trusted Lee because his own encryption key was "signed" by several prominent agitators for Internet privacy. Lee checked in with Poitras: was it okay to send her e-mail and encryption key to a stranger who said he had valuable information to share? With Poitras's permission, Lee gave his anonymous contact (Snowden)the information, setting the stage for numerous groundbreaking revelations about the depth and breadth of the intelligence community's surveillance capabilities.

None of this could have happened without several overlapping communities: the community of people who use a certain type of encrypted e-mail that included Snowden, Lee, and Poitras; the community of privacy advocates that welcomed Lee into their ranks; and the community of people who work to protect journalists' ability to report safely (the Freedom of the Press Foundation) and which brought Lee and Poitras together. These days, Lee is part of our communities, too: he

---

70. https://theintercept.com/2014/10/28/smuggling-snowden-secrets/.

worked with Talya at the Intercept and with Alison at the Tor Project. For us, this story—which we viewed from afar as it unfolded as a tale of black-cloaked intrigue—now feels less like a story about subterfuge and more like one about friends-of-friends, about people with shared interests and values who work to keep each other safe and to empower each other. That's how we must approach it in libraries, too.

Early in this discussion, we described anonymity as "herd immunity." You can't send a secure message into the void; you need someone on the other end who has the tools to receive it securely. Technologists can invent all kinds of protocols and programs, but until people adopt them and use them together, these privacy mechanisms will fall into irrelevance.

A library physically manifests a community of trust. People trust the library to provide free information and resources, without bias, to anyone who walks in the door. Of course, inequitable community power dynamics and unexamined biases can cause many libraries to fall short of this ideal. But what if we try harder to live up to it? What if we take our library community as a starting place for expanding awareness of anti-surveillance, privacy, and anonymity-defending practices?

Around the United States, communities find their resolve to stay together being tested in the face of regular surveillance. The journalist Assia Boundaoui grew up in Bridgeview, Illinois, where the predominantly Muslim community was subject to decades-long (and likely ongoing) FBI surveillance. Her documentary *The Feeling of Being Watched* chronicles both her efforts to obtain the FBI's records of its years of watching the community and her attempts to get her neighbors to talk about what they've experienced and how they've felt as a result of years of knowing they were being watched.[71] "The problem with surveillance is that it really gets its power from secrecy, and when FBI agents came and knocked on people's doors, they reacted in fear," she says.

> We've been trying to convince people that the way to fight this is to be really open and public about it, because it didn't just happen to you, it also happened to the person next door and the person down the street. There's a power in this collective story, and we have to stop being afraid. We're already on a list, so it's not as if we speak out, we're going to be added to one. Being quiet about it has never kept anyone in our community safe.[72]

A public institution that openly resists the normalizing of surveillance, that opens up a conversation about a topic that feels daunting or scary to discuss openly, that empowers people to maintain their ability to learn without the fear of being watched, can help bring people together. Libraries have come to be a place where communities meet in moments of crisis; we pride ourselves on keeping our doors open when our communities need us, as we did in Baltimore and Ferguson. We are all, collectively in a time of digital emergency: fake news, threats to net neutrality, ubiquitous government surveillance, and constant corporate incursions on our identities, which we're increasingly forced to leak out online in bits and streams. No one is better situated to bring people together to learn about and fight these forces than librarians.

71. http://www.feelingofbeingwatched.com/.
72. https://www.wbez.org/shows/worldview/the-feeling-of-being-watched-filmmaker-on-fbi-surveillance-of-muslims-in-bridgeview-illinois/0dc248f0-b878-495c-a44f-199efab6c273.

NOTES AND RESOURCES

IT'S AN UNDERSTATEMENT TO SAY THAT ISSUES SURROUNDING privacy, anonymity, and surveillance are a moving target. In the time since we began writing this book, there have been changes in surveillance law, a few big-name data breaches, and major developments in the Facebook-Cambridge Analytica scandal, which has prompted Facebook to make big promises about improving its data privacy practices. Here are a few websites that offer evergreen resources that we recommend.

Library Freedom Project and Library Freedom Institute

LFP makes real the promise of intellectual freedom in libraries by teaching librarians about surveillance threats, privacy rights, and technology for digital liberation. Library Freedom Institute is LFP's intensive four- to six-month training program to turn librarians into full-on privacy advocates. Learn more at libraryfreedomproject.org and libraryfreedomproject.org/lfi.

Electronic Frontier Foundation

In addition to being a reliable source of news about digital security and privacy and freedom of speech issues, the EFF has created two invaluable guides:

- Security Education Companion (https://sec.eff.org/) provides a curriculum for people teaching classes about digital privacy and security, complete with teaching materials and a syllabus.
- Surveillance Self-Defense (https://ssd.eff.org) provides an in-depth guide to thinking about digital security based on a number of different threat models. It's also available in a number of languages.

Access Now

Access Now offers a Digital Security Helpline for activists, journalists, and others who feel they are at risk and need digital security assistance. Their "A First Look at Digital Security" pamphlet is an accessible and engaging way to get people thinking about threat modeling. See https://www.accessnow.org/cms/assets/uploads/2018/03/A-first-look-at-digital-security-digital-copy.pdf.

Tor Project

Download the Tor Browser and find resources about Tor, onion services, and more at https://www.torproject.org/projects/torbrowser.html.

Onionshare

Download the secure file-transfer tool Onionshare at https://onionshare.org/.

Lucy Parsons Labs

https://lucyparsonslabs.com/

Lucy Parsons Labs is a Chicago-based nonprofit and advocacy organization dedicated to the "intersection of digital rights and on-the-streets issues." Through digital security education events, Freedom of Information Act activism, and data science projects, their work straddles both the low-tech surveillance that citizens experience in their daily lives and the high-tech tools that broaden the reach of this surveillance.

Crash Override Network

www.crashoverridenetwork.com

The Crash Override Network is an organization that provides support and resources for people who are experiencing online harassment and abuse. It has several particularly useful guides for people who feel at risk of or who have already been doxed.

WITNESS
www.witness.org

WITNESS supports activists worldwide who create video documentation of human rights abuses. Both within and outside of that context, this organization has compiled several guides about documenting police and other human rights abuses, and preserving and archiving digital videos and other technology; these guides are essential primers for handling digital materials securely.

Tactical Technology Collective
https://tacticaltech.org/

This Berlin-based group aims to "address how data and digital technologies impact human rights, social justice, power structures, and accountability." They conduct research, with an activist focus, into how technology affects democracy, and have created a slew of training and educational materials. We discussed their "Data Detox Kit" earlier; this is a clear, easy-to-follow resource that helps a person realize how many traces she's left all over the Web and how companies track her.

Riseup.net
https://www.riseup.net

Riseup.net offers safer communication tools, including e-mail (and e-mail storage), chat, VPN (virtual private network) services, and mailing lists that can be used by community and activist groups. You need an invitation from another Riseup user to create an account. Protonmail is another service that offers safer e-mail.

Freedom of the Press Foundation
https://freedom.press

The Freedom of the Press Foundation supports journalists and whistleblowers, particularly those whose work exposes government and corporate malfeasance. To that end, they do First Amendment advocacy, create tools like SecureDrop (available at SecureDrop.org), and also offer training and security resources, including a useful guide to choosing a VPN service.

The Guardian Project
https://guardianproject.info/

The Guardian Project is an international nonprofit that focuses on creating mobile apps that journalists and human rights defenders can use to document major events securely and verifiably, and skirt Internet censorship. They collaborate with some of the other organizations we've discussed, including the Tor Project and WITNESS.

ALA Privacy Checklists
http://www.ala.org/advocacy/privacy/checklists

The Library Privacy Checklists, drafted by the IFC Privacy Subcommittee and the LITA Patron Privacy Interest Group, are intended to provide libraries of all types with practical guidance on implementing the Library Privacy Guidelines[73] published by the Intellectual Freedom Committee in 2016. These checklists are supremely helpful in minimizing and securing data, which are necessary steps to helping make your library more anonymity-friendly.

---

73. http://www.ala.org/advocacy/privacy/guidelines.